Quick Activities to Build a Very

VOLUMINOUS VOCABULARY

by LeAnn Nickelsen

SCHOLASTIC

PROFESSIONAL BOOKS

NEW YORK • TORONTO • LONDON • AUCKLAND • SYDNEY

MEXICO CITY • NEW DELHI • HONG KONG

Thank you to:

- Grapevine-Colleyville ISD in Texas for providing the resources and classes that were needed to write this book.

- Dr. McWhorter, my professor, and Anne Simpson, our district's Language Arts Coordinator, for providing ideas, resources, and editing.

- Karen and Russ Biggs for their computer help! You computer geniuses!

- Dove Elementary staff for their ideas, resources, and encouragement. You're an awesome staff to work with!

I dedicate this book to my parents, Jim and Dolores Heim, who encouraged me to be a teacher and to my helpful, loving, encouraging, giving husband, Joel, who kept up with all of my other duties while I finished this book. I could not have done it without you all. I love you!

Cover design by Jaime Lucero and Vincent Ceci
Interior design by Kathy Massaro

ISBN 0-590-22179-5

Contents

Introduction

Why Is Teaching Vocabulary Important?

In my classroom, I have noticed students having great difficulty understanding a reading assignment when they encounter a few unknown words. In order to fully comprehend reading material, students must possess both decoding skills and vocabulary knowledge.

Vocabulary knowledge refers not only to the understanding of the key words in a text, but also students' understanding of overall ideas and concepts being communicated. For example, in order to understand a passage about the solar system, students must be familiar with the meaning of words such as *satellite* and *orbit*. Beyond these words, students need to grasp the encompassing concept of solar system. The more vocabulary words students know, the better their comprehension.

In addition to contributing to reading comprehension, developing students' vocabulary can increase their speaking and writing skills, improve their scores on standardized tests, and teach specific concepts in content areas.

What Works and Doesn't Work in Vocabulary Instruction

When I discovered that vocabulary was crucial to reading comprehension, I set out to find the best strategies and activities to increase my students' vocabulary. Unfortunately, not all vocabulary instruction increases comprehension. As William Nagy states in his book *Teaching Vocabulary to Improve Reading Comprehension*: "Explicit vocabulary instruction is not very effective at producing substantial gains in overall vocabulary size or in reading comprehension." Nagy goes on to say: "It appears that the following are attributes which can make vocabulary instruction effective at increasing reading comprehension: multiple exposures to words, exposure to words in meaningful contexts, rich or varied information about each word, establishment of ties between words and students' own experience and prior knowledge, and an active role by students in the word-learning process."

According to research there are three key components to effective vocabulary instruction: **integration, repetition,** and **meaningful use.** Instruction that combines these elements is the most effective method of improving vocabulary.

Integration: The first element of effective vocabulary instruction is connecting new vocabulary words to each other, to the curriculum, and to students' prior knowledge. Students are better able to learn and remember sets of words that are connected by theme or subject than an unorganized list of words.

Repetition: The second property of effective vocabulary instruction is repetition. Repeatedly exposing students to vocabulary words will allow students to retain the meaning, so that when they encounter the word again they remember it.

Meaningful Use: Finally, students need to use vocabulary words in a meaningful, active way to full comprehend them.

Organizing Classroom Time to Include Vocabulary Instruction

If you're like me, you want to know the best way to organize or manage your class time in order to produce the most literate students. By taking into account all of the research and incorporating the qualities of effective vocabulary instruction, I developed a system that works well in my classroom: it's a whole literacy approach in which vocabulary skills are gained in a variety of ways. Here are my strategies for vocabulary instruction.

Schedule class time for silent reading and reading aloud. Teach students to use context clues to identify unknown words.

Students' vocabulary grows tremendously when they read independently and when they hear stories and novels read aloud. To make this exposure to new words as beneficial as possible, I teach students to use context clues to discern the meaning of unknown words. In Part 1 of this book, you'll find a lesson plan for teaching students to interpret context clues, as well as other strategies students can use when they encounter new words.

Develop vocabulary lists from the novels and texts you will be reading in class.

I choose all vocabulary for instruction from novels, textbooks, and curriculum themes that we will be studying in class. As I plan a unit or start a new book, I select twenty to thirty vocabulary words that students will need to know to understand a new unit or text. This improves students' reading comprehension and, since they will encounter the words throughout a unit, also helps them remember the words.

Before reading new material, pre-teach students important words to help them comprehend the material.

I often plan pre-reading activities for new reading materials to help prepare students for any difficult words they will encounter. In fact, when I introduce students to words before reading, they are often excited when they come across the word and try to guess the meaning using context clues. Part 1 features pre-reading activities to help you introduce new words to students.

Organize targeted lessons and short activities to give students the opportunity to study new words, learn vocabulary strategies, and put new words to use.

Targeted lessons are an ideal way to help students learn words that are more conceptual and difficult to understand. For example, while reading *Maniac Magee* students needed to understand the vague concepts of *discrimination*, *racism*, and *prejudice*. These are very difficult, abstract words for a 5th grader to comprehend and a targeted lesson can create a fuller, richer understanding of these vocabulary words. Look for vocabulary mini-lessons and activities in Part 2 and ways to write with new vocabulary words in Part 3.

 Incorporate graphic organizers into vocabulary units to help students learn new words.

Graphic organizers are an effective way to get students to think about a word in new and different ways and to organize their thinking. You'll find ideas for graphic organizers in Part 4.

 Spend time reviewing vocabulary words.

Research has shown that in addition to learning words in context, students must be repeatedly exposed to words to truly retain them. In Part 5, I've included games and other activities to give you and your students many different ways to review vocabulary words.

PART 1

Adjacent
Aficionado
Auspicious

Barter
Benevolent
Buoyant

Cauldron
Cantankerous
Clamor

Dabble
Density
Dismantle

Earnest
Ebullience
Extrovert

Integrating Vocabulary Instruction Into Your Reading Program

Pre-Reading and Post-Reading Activities

Reading Roles: Vocabulary Enricher

OBJECTIVE: Integrate vocabulary instruction into reading groups.

GROUPING: Small groups of 4 to 5 students.

What to Do

I have incorporated vocabulary instruction into both whole class reading instruction and small reading groups. I schedule a two-hour period for reading. For the first 20 minutes, I teach a whole class lesson. I use this time to teach vocabulary mini-lessons, to review context clues strategies, or to pre-teach new vocabulary words to students.

After the whole class lesson, students meet in small reading groups. Each student in the group is assigned one of the reading roles listed below, with one student responsible for new words. I frequently assign new roles, so everyone has a chance to play every role.

Literary Luminary: Identifies two passages in the text to discuss or read aloud. The passages might be funny, exciting, or confusing, or it might include examples of literary devices such as similes or metaphors.

 Discussion Director: Prepares five questions about the assigned reading. The questions need to be more than simply "what" questions.

 Summary Sleuth: Writes a brief summary of the text including the setting, important events, problems, setting, and characters.

 Vocabulary Enricher: Selects five new words in the text, finds definitions for the words and then shares the words with their group. As a follow-up, the group can write new sentences using the words. To help students with this task, reproduce the form on page 15.

Teaching Students to Use Context Clues

Whether it's called DEAR time or sustained silent reading, a popular trend in schools today is to allocate more time to in-school reading. As students increase the amount of independent reading they do, they dramatically increase the amount of new words they encounter. Educators Jane Buikema and Michael Graves investigated the idea of teaching students how to use context clues to comprehend new words and created a lesson plan designed to teach students how to recognize and use context clues to understand unfamiliar words. I have adapted the five-day lesson plan that Buikmea and Graves designed into the following three-day lesson plan. I used it with my fifth-grade students and saw my students using context to accurately predict word meanings. I also saw state standardized test scores in reading improve greatly.

Day 1: Riddle Clues

OBJECTIVE: Students find clues that help them solve a word riddle.

What to Do

1. Read the following riddle aloud and ask students to guess what the answer is:

I am a color which symbolizes wealth. I am often seen on the robes of queens and kings. I am also on petals of flowers. What am I?

ANSWER: purple

2. Once students guess the answer, ask them to point out any clues or cues that gave the answer away.

Follow-Up Activity

Ask students to write or find a riddle to share on the following day.

Day 2: How to Find the Context Clues

OBJECTIVE: Students relate the similarities between solving word riddles and inferring unknown word meanings from context.

What to Do

1. Begin by having students share the riddles they have collected. As you solve the riddles in class, discuss with students how the clues in each riddle help you find the answer.

2. Explain to students that context clues, like the clues in a riddle, are the clues in the text that can help them understand an unknown word.

3. Put the first sample passage from the Context Clues reproducible (page 16) on the overhead or hand out copies of the page.

4. Ask students to read the passage and underline the unknown words. (The word *sandwich* has been replaced with *wertbet*)

5. Next, ask students to look for clues in the text that help reveal the meaning of the word.

6. Using the clues they have identified, ask students to predict the meaning of the word.

7. Repeat the same procedure with the remaining passages. The mystery words in the second and third passages are *computer* and *apples*, respectively. The fourth passage features real words, *pachyderms, foliage,* and *prehensile,* for students to work with.

Follow-Up Activity

Students apply what they have learned by finding two unknown words in a book they are currently reading and using the steps above to figure out what the words mean.

Day 3: Context Clue Practice

OBJECTIVE: Students define an unknown word by evaluating context clues around the word.

What to Do

1. Review the steps you take to find context clues in a reading passage.

2. Ask students to look through the dictionary to find an unknown word. Then have each student write a short passage, similar to the ones on the reproducible, using an unknown word and adding clues to the word's meaning.

3. Have students exchanges passages with other students and attempt to figure out the unknown words in their classmates' work.

Follow-Up Activity

To give students additional practice, you might create additional passages for students to work on independently.

Cloze Activity

OBJECTIVE: To determine their background knowledge about a particular subject, students fill in missing words in a reading passage.
GROUPING: Individual

A cloze activity is a good way to determine how much students already know about a topic before you start a new unit or study. To create a cloze exercise, delete approximately 10 to 15 significant vocabulary words from a 250-word passage. Provide students with a list of the missing words and ask them to fill in the blanks with the correct words. As you review the correct answers with students, you will be able to identify which words and concepts are familiar to students and which are unfamiliar.

Word Wonder

OBJECTIVE: In this pre-reading activity, students use their prior knowledge to predict if vocabulary words will be included in a reading assignment.

GROUPING: Individuals or small groups

What to Do

Before beginning a new reading assignment, present students with a list of vocabulary words related to the reading assignment. Challenge students to look carefully at the list of words and predict if each word will or will not be in the passage. Students may look at the book cover and title for clues. If students decide that the word will be included, they should write a short definition for the word. If students decide the word will not be included, they should write "no" next to it. After students have completed the reading, review the list as a class, discuss the accuracy of student's predictions, and share the definitions of any unfamiliar words.

Vocabulary Inventory

OBJECTIVE: To help students identify which words they need to work with, students sort words according to how well they know them.

GROUPING: Individuals or small groups

What to Do

Pass out copies of the Vocabulary Inventory on page 17. Have students sort the vocabulary words on their current word list or from a recent reading assignment into three categories: Words I Know Well, Words I Have Seen Before, and Words I Don't Know. After the list is generated, students can use any of the activities in Part 2, such as the Vocabulary Cube, to learn the words they don't know well.

Connect Two

OBJECTIVE: Students pick any two words from a new vocabulary list and connect them together in a sentence.

GROUPING: Partners

What to Do

Write each new vocabulary word on a slip of paper and give each student a word. Then, assign each student a partner and challenge the pairs to find a relationship between their words and write a sentence using the words. They can look up words in the dictionary. For example, students might connect the words antelope and thicket with the sentence: The antelope hid in the thicket.

Predict-o-Gram

OBJECTIVE: Students predict where each vocabulary word will be found in a story: in the setting, with a character, to describe an action, or as a describing word.

GROUPING: Small groups

What to Do

Use the Predict-o-Gram to introduce students to the vocabulary words they will encounter in a book chapter or novel. Hand out copies of the Predict-o-Gram on page 18, along with the list of vocabulary words. Divide the class into small groups and explain to students that their goal is to predict where each word on the vocabulary list will be used in the story. After completing the book or chapter, have each group review their Predict-o-Gram, reevaluate where each word belongs, and make a new Predict-o-Gram.

Word Study

OBJECTIVE: Prepare students for new words they will encounter in a novel or story by having them select two words to study in great depth.

GROUPING: Individual

What to Do

Pick out 20–40 words that you want students to learn from a novel you will be reading in class. Write each word on an index card or a slip of paper and place all the words in a large envelope. Have each student pick two words from the envelope and, using the reproducible on page 19, complete a Word Study for each word. Students begin by writing down what they think the word means. Next, they confirm the definition in the dictionary and use a thesaurus to find synonyms and antonyms for the word. Finally, they use the word in a sentence and draw a picture that illustrates the meaning of the word.

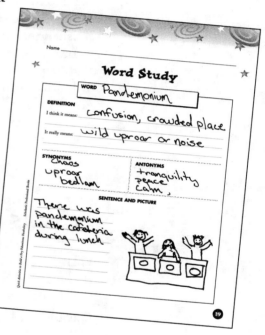

After students have completed their word studies, collect them and place the words in the order that they will appear in the novel you will be reading. As you begin each chapter in the book, display the Word Studies for words that will appear in that chapter. Students can then refer to them as they read. When you have finished reading, bind all of the pages together into a book students can refer to in the future.

Flagging New Words

OBJECTIVE: Students mark difficult words in a reading passage with self-sticking note paper.

GROUPING: Individual

What to Do

During silent reading, give students self-sticking notepads to mark words that they don't understand. Then, students can select two or three of the words and use the reproducible on page 19 to complete a Word Study for each word.

Vocabulary Journals

OBJECTIVE: Students create a personal journal of vocabulary words.

GROUPING: Individual

What to Do

Invite students to designate one notebook as their vocabulary journal. Students can create a journal entry for any new or unfamiliar words they come across when they are reading. In each journal entry, students can include the sentence the word was used in and what they think the word means (based on context clues). They can complete the entry, after they have finished reading, by looking the word up in the dictionary and writing down a correct definition. If applicable, they can add an illustration or diagram that helps to define the word.

Journals can also be a great place to take notes about difficult concepts. A great way for students to take notes is to divide each page into two columns and take notes in one column and draw a picture in the other column.

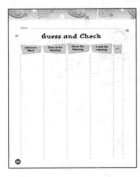

Guess and Check Chart

OBJECTIVE: Use a Guess and Check Chart to encourage students to deduce the meaning of a word by examining the context clues around the word and then check to see if their guess was correct.

GROUPING: Individual

What to Do

The Guess and Check Chart is an easy way to reinforce the skill of using context clues while reading. Before students tackle new reading materials, hand out copies of the reproducible on page 20. As students read, they should write down any new or unfamiliar words in the first column and any clues to the word's meaning in the second column. In the third column, they should "guess" what the word means. After they have finished reading, students should complete the final column by looking up each word in the dictionary. Reviewing students' Guess and Check Charts as a class is a great opportunity for students to share the strategies they use to figure out difficult words.

Vocabulary Enricher

Use the spaces below to write down any new words you come across as you read. Write down the sentence the word was used in, as well as the definition. Then try to use the word in a sentence of your own.

Word: _____ Sentence in book: _____
_____

Definition: _____
New sentence: _____
_____

Word: _____ Sentence in book: _____
_____

Definition: _____
New sentence: _____
_____

Word: _____ Sentence in book: _____
_____

Definition: _____
New sentence: _____
_____

Word: _____ Sentence in book: _____
_____

Definition: _____
New sentence: _____
_____

Word: _____ Sentence in book: _____
_____

Definition: _____
New sentence: _____
_____

Context Clues

Steps for identifying unknown words:

1. Underline any word you don't know in the passage.

2. Identify any words or phrases from the passage that are clues to the meaning of the word.

3. Predict what the word means.

The wertbet Sam brought for lunch looked delicious. It had layers of roast beef, cheese, lettuce, and tomato—all piled between two slices of bread. Sam couldn't wait to eat it.

The heavy, expensive cloccloey is very useful in the classroom. Students actually fight over whose turn it is to use it. Research, typing, games, and other activities are done on it.

Tanya loved to pick pyrus in the fall. She would pick bushels of the red fruit and use them to make pies, muffins, and other sweets.

This type of pachyderm lives in both Asia and Africa. These enormous animals feast on foliage and use their long, prehensile trunks to drink water and pick up food. In parts of Asia and India, they are trained to work for humans, carrying loads, lifting, and moving objects.

Quick Activities to Build a Very Voluminous Vocabulary   Scholastic Professional Books

Name _____

Vocabulary Inventory

Words I Know Well	Words I Have Seen Before (I think I know the meaning)	Words I Don't Know

Quick Activities to Build a Very Voluminous Vocabulary   Scholastic Professional Books

Name _____

Predict-o-Gram

Setting:

_____
_____
_____
_____
_____

Characters:

_____
_____
_____
_____
_____
_____

Action (Problem):

_____
_____
_____
_____
_____

Describing Words:

_____
_____
_____
_____
_____
_____

Other:

_____
_____
_____
_____
_____

Quick Activities to Build a Very Voluminous Vocabulary

Scholastic Professional Books

Name _____

Word Study

WORD

DEFINITION

I think it means: ....
....

It really means: ....
....

SYNONYMS

ANTONYMS

SENTENCE AND PICTURE

Guess and Check

Unknown Word	Clues to the Meaning	Guess the Meaning	Check the Meaning	+/-

Quick Activities to Build a Very Voluminous Vocabulary   Scholastic Professional Books

PART 2

F
Fiasco
Finite
Flamboyant

G
Gallantry
Genial
Gimmick

H
Huckster
Hologram
Hierarchy

I
Insipid
Ingratiate
Incumbent

J
Jocular
Jumble
Jaunty

Learning New Vocabulary

Understanding New Words and Building Vocabulary

Synonym Webs

OBJECTIVE: Stretch students' writing vocabulary by creating Synonym Webs for overused words.

GROUPING: Whole class

What to Do

Students often get in the habit of using the same words over and over again. To encourage them to branch out, trying building Synonym Webs. Determine which words you think students overuse and then, as a class, brainstorm synonyms. For example, my students tend to use the word nice too much. We came up with as many alternatives as possible and created a Word Cone for students to refer to when they are writing. Other ideas for Synonym Webs might include a Rainbow of Words, a Chain of Words, or a simple Word Web. Students can continue to add to their Synonym Webs as they learn new words.

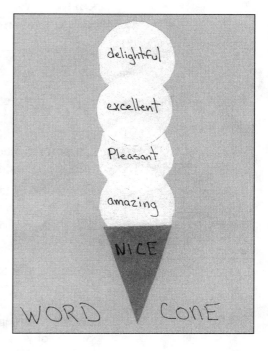

delightful

excellent

Pleasant

amazing

NICE

WORD CONE

Sentence Starters

OBJECTIVE: Students embed vocabulary words in complex sentences.

GROUPING: Whole class

What to Do

Try this activity to encourage students to use a variety of sentence structures in their writing and give them an opportunity to put new vocabulary to work. Start by writing the first part of a sentence using a vocabulary word. You can make the sentence starter an independent clause, a dependent clause, a prepositional phrase, or any other type of sentence structure you would like your students to use. For extra motivation, personalize the sentence starters by incorporating references to familiar people, places, or events.

Display the sentence starters, along with a list of additional vocabulary words, on an overhead transparency. Ask students to complete each sentence using one of the vocabulary words. Be sure to have students share their sentences with the class.

EXAMPLES:

While Stephanie toiled furiously to repair the spaceship, _____.

While on our arduous journey to the mountain, _____.

I ransacked the house looking for the report and Sue _____.

In addition to being an avid bowler, Tyrone_____.

On top of the spiral staircase _____.

Sam is so obstinate that _____.

_____is a student who_____.

Word Pyramid

OBJECTIVE: Students define a word with synonyms, antonyms, adjectives, and a sentence.

GROUPING: Individual or partners

What to Do

Word Pyramids are another method of guiding students as they define a word. Reproduce copies of the Word Pyramid on page 28 and explain to students that they are going to use a Word Pyramid to define a word. To create the pyramid, students complete the first line with the word, the second line with two antonyms, and the third line with three synonyms. In line four, students add four describing words. In line five they use the word in a sentence.

Facts and Feelings Pyramid

OBJECTIVE: Students list facts about a word in pyramid form.

GROUPING: Individual

What to Do

Facts and Feelings Pyramids, like Word Pyramids, are another way for students to summarize their knowledge. Students start the pyramid with the word they are studying. On the second line they write a two-word phrase that expresses how they feel about the word. In the following lines, they use progressively longer phrases to list facts they know about the word.

> ## Meteorologists
>
> Very helpful
>
> Study the weather
>
> Predict rain, wind, and snow
>
> Use thermometers, barometers, maps, & anemometers

Changing Parts of Speech

OBJECTIVE: Students learn how words can operate as different parts of speech and analyze how the meaning of a word can change based on how it is used in a sentence.

GROUPING: Whole class and individual

What to Do

Students begin this activity by selecting five new vocabulary words that they have encountered in a novel or text you are reading in class. Students write down the sentence the word was used in and determine what part of speech the word is. Then, using a dictionary for reference, students write a sentence using the word as a different part of speech. Remind students that in some cases changing the part of speech might change the meaning of the word. Students can complete this activity using the reproducible on page 29.

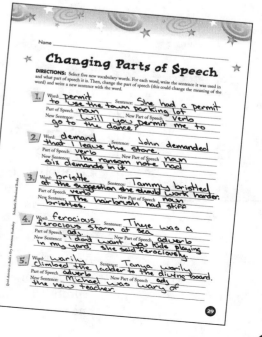

Prefix and Suffix Webs

OBJECTIVE: Students learn common prefixes, suffixes, and root words.

GROUPING: Whole class and individual

What to Do

Knowing the meaning of different prefixes and suffixes can help students unlock the meaning of new or unfamiliar words. Every Tuesday morning I introduce a new affix to my class. I begin by writing the prefix or suffix on the board. Then, using the reproducible graphic organizer on page 30, I ask students to brainstorm words with that particular prefix or suffix. After students have completed the web, we share the words we have brainstormed and discuss how the prefix or suffix gives meaning to each word. Students keep their prefix and suffix webs in their folders to use as a resource throughout the year. To get started, look for the list of 50 common affixes on page 62. You can also copy the list for students and invite them to add to the list.

Easy Category Review

OBJECTIVE: Students review the meaning of vocabulary words as they sort them into categories.

GROUPING: Individual and small groups

What to Do

At the end of a unit, students can review vocabulary words by sorting them into categories based on what type of word they are. Hand out copies of the reproducible on page 31 and ask students to place each vocabulary word in one of the following categories:

1. **Personal:** Words that can describe a person's personality, background, beliefs, values, or appearance. (adjectives)

2. **Action:** Words that can be displayed, exhibited, or acted out. (feelings or action verbs)

3. **Example:** Words that can be explained using an example.

4. **Illustrate:** Words that can be explained with a picture.

5. **Definition:** Words that can only be explained by using the definition. (You won't have many of these.)

Once students have completed this task, review everyone's choices and decide as a class the best category for each word. Next, divide the students into five groups and assign each group a category. The groups must then define all of the words in their category in the appropriate fashion. For example, students with action words must act out the meaning of the words, while students with words in the illustrate category must use visual aids to define the words.

Vocabulary Cube

OBJECTIVE: Students analyze, define, apply, compare, and evaluate a word when they make a Vocabulary Cube.

GROUPING: Individual

What to Do

Hand out copies of the Vocabulary Cube on page 32 to students. Have students complete the cube by filling in each side.

1. **Analyze the word:** List the part of the speech, root word, prefix, or suffix.

2. **Define the word:** Write a brief definition.

3. **Apply the word:** What can you do with it?

4. **Compare the word:** What is it similar to or different from? List any synonyms or antonyms.

5. **Argue the word:** Make an opinion statement using this word and argue for or against it.

6. **Associate the word:** How is this word related to your life? What does it make you think of?

After students have completed the cube, they can assemble it by following the directions on the reproducible. Display the Vocabulary Cubes around the room for everyone to see.

Relationship Chart

OBJECTIVE: Students make connections between vocabulary and the major ideas or themes in a text.

GROUPING: Whole class and individual

To create a Relationship Chart, write four or five of the important ideas or major themes from the text across the top of the chart on page 33. List important vocabulary words from the text down the side.

Students complete the chart by looking at each vocabulary word and determining if it is related in any way to the important ideas in the text. For example, in a reading about the Pilgrims, students might learn new words such as separatists, merchants, and strangers. As they complete the Relationship Chart, they must decide if the words are related to the major ideas in the text, such as "freedom of religion" or "desire to own land." Students can place a check mark in the box if the word is related.

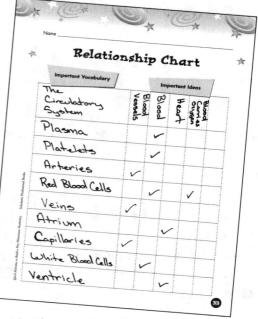

Synonym Wheels

OBJECTIVE: Students eliminate the word that doesn't belong in a group of synonyms and then place the word in the correct group.

GROUPING: Individual

To create Synonym Wheels, you'll need four sets of six synonyms and a copy of the reproducible on page 34. Select one group of synonyms and write five of the words in one circle. Place the sixth word in another circle. Continue this until all the circles are filled in with five synonyms and one word that doesn't belong. Make copies of the reproducible and hand out to your class. Ask students to underline the word in each circle that doesn't belong. Then they should find where each missing word belongs and write it underneath the correct circle.

Synonym Gradient

OBJECTIVE: Students learn to identify precise meanings and distinguish between different words by ranking a list of synonyms.

GROUPING: Individual or small groups

What to Do

Present students with a list of words that have similar meanings. According to the nature of the word, come up with two extremes and, as a class, rank the synonyms based on these extremes. For example, if your list includes the words blaring, deafening, earsplitting, and boisterous, you might have students rank the words from loud to loudest.

Creating Analogies

OBJECTIVE: Students develop their higher-order thinking skills and demonstrate word knowledge when they create analogies with their vocabulary words.

GROUPING: Partners

What to Do

We often use analogies when we compare known words to unknown words, and working with analogies in a formal manner is an effective way for students to understand new words. The reproducible on page 35 shows eight basic analogy constructions. Reproduce How to Create an Analogy and share with students. Review each type of analogy together and, as a class, brainstorm new examples of analogies. Once student understand the concept, you can apply analogies to your vocabulary words in the following ways.

☆ Start analogies that students must finish.

☆ Present the answers to complete the analogies in multiple choice format.

☆ Have students start an analogy for another student to complete.

Word Pyramid

_____
WORD

_____ _____
ANTONYMS

_____ _____ _____
SYNONYMS

_____ _____ _____ _____
ADJECTIVES DESCRIBING THE WORD

_____
WRITE A SENTENCE USING THE WORD

_____

Quick Activities to Build a Very Voluminous Vocabulary

Scholastic Professional Books

Name _____

Changing Parts of Speech

DIRECTIONS: Select five new vocabulary words. For each word, write the sentence it was used in and what part of speech it is. Then, change the part of speech (this could change the meaning of the word) and write a new sentence with the word.

1. Word:_____ Sentence: _____

_____

Part of Speech_____ New Part of Speech _____

New Sentence: _____

_____

2. Word:_____ Sentence: _____

_____

Part of Speech_____ New Part of Speech _____

New Sentence: _____

_____

3. Word:_____ Sentence: _____

_____

Part of Speech_____ New Part of Speech _____

New Sentence: _____

_____

4. Word:_____ Sentence: _____

_____

Part of Speech_____ New Part of Speech _____

New Sentence: _____

_____

5. Word:_____ Sentence: _____

_____

Part of Speech_____ New Part of Speech _____

New Sentence: _____

_____

Name _____

Prefix and Suffix Web

Quick Activities to Build a Very Voluminous Vocabulary

Scholastic Professional Books

Word Categories

Name _____

Definition	Illustrate	Example	Action	Personal

Vocabulary Cube

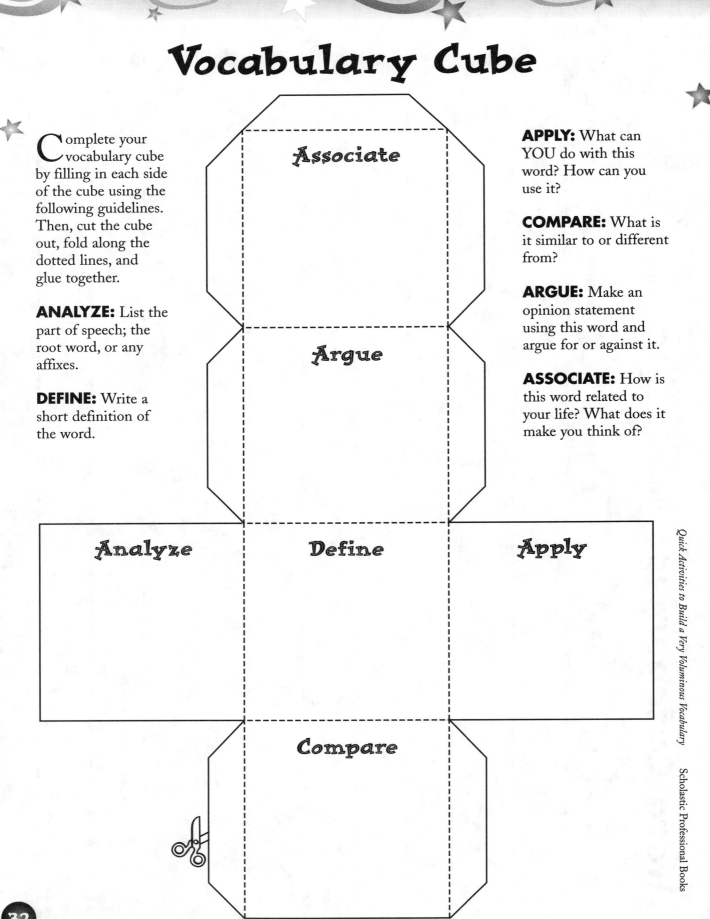

Complete your vocabulary cube by filling in each side of the cube using the following guidelines. Then, cut the cube out, fold along the dotted lines, and glue together.

ANALYZE: List the part of speech; the root word, or any affixes.

DEFINE: Write a short definition of the word.

APPLY: What can YOU do with this word? How can you use it?

COMPARE: What is it similar to or different from?

ARGUE: Make an opinion statement using this word and argue for or against it.

ASSOCIATE: How is this word related to your life? What does it make you think of?

Associate

Argue

Analyze   Define   Apply

Compare

Quick Activities to Build a Very Voluminous Vocabulary

Scholastic Professional Books

Name _____

Relationship Chart

Important Vocabulary	Important Ideas			

Synonym Wheels

Find the word in each circle that doesn't belong. Underline it and then write the word under the circle group where it does belong.

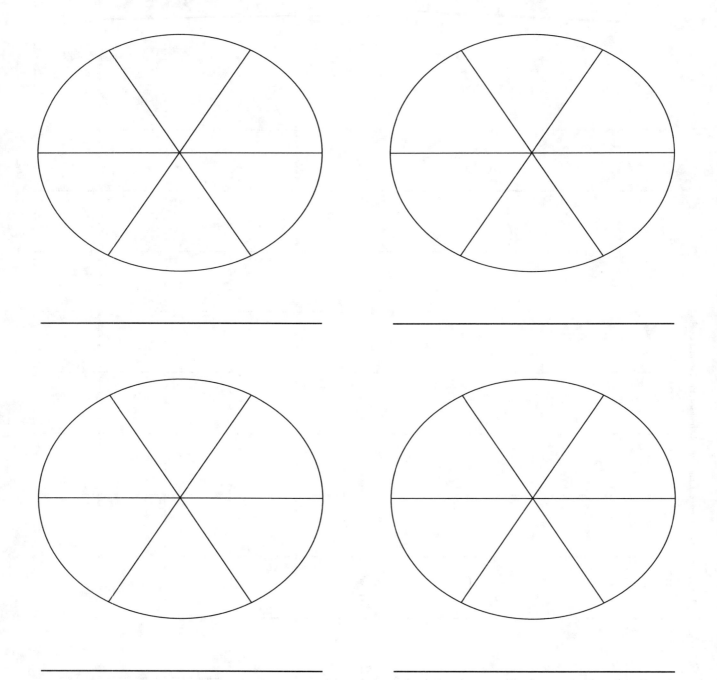

Quick Activities to Build a Very Voluminous Vocabulary

Scholastic Professional Books

How To Create an Analogy

Here are examples of different kinds of analogies.

 Similar Concepts
Adjacent concepts that are synonyms or similar in meaning.

Example: *jump : leap :: shout : scream*

 Dissimilar Concepts
Adjacent concepts that are antonyms or dissimilar in meaning.

Example: *this : that :: go : come*

 Class Membership
Adjacent concepts that belong to the same class or category.

Example: *elephant : lion :: blue : pink*

Class Name and Class Member
One element in a set is a class name while the other is a member of the class.

Example: *fork : utensil :: bee : insect*

Part to Whole
One element in a set is a part of the other element in the set.

Example: *wheel : car :: heel : leg*

 Change
One element in a set turns into the other element.

Example: *plant : seed :: caterpillar : butterfly*

 Function
One element in a set performs a function on or for another.

Example: *tutor : student :: driver : car*

 Quantity/Size
The two elements in the set are comparable in terms of quantity or size.

Example: *valley : hole :: lion : house cat*

Quick Activities to Build a Very Voluminous Vocabulary   Scholastic Professional Books

PART 3

K — Kindred Kiosk Kudos

L — Labyrinth Lenient Loquacious

M — Magnanimous Meager Microcosm

N — Nadir Naive Nefarious

O — Obelisk Opulent Ostentatious

Writing With Vocabulary Words

Activities to Put New Words to Work

Word Stories

OBJECTIVE: Students remember a word's meaning by writing a story about the word.

GROUPING: Individual

What to Do

This activity was inspired by Paul M. Levitt's *The Weighty Word Book* (Manuscripts Ltd. 1985), which defines words with short stories that incorporate the meaning of the word into the story. For example, the book defines the word expedient by telling the story of an ant that used to be quick and speedy when searching for food. Then one day he discovered a picnic area that provided an endless supply of tasty tidbits. Since he found a better way to solve this problem and no longer had to be quick to find food, he became the "ex-speedy ant." Share examples from the book and then challenge students to write and illustrate their own word stories. Students can use this technique with words they are having trouble understanding. After students have finished, read everyone's story aloud and then bind them together to make your own *Word Stories* book.

> How Inauguration came to be
>
> Once upon a time there was a girl named UR. This was short for Ursula Rose. She loved everything and anything to do with horses. She owned her own horse named Stardust. Stardust was pregnant with a foal in August. Well, Ursula Rose just loved Stardust to pieces. UR knew her foal would be beautiful. But her dad had another view of it. He said UR had take care of it. and if she did not do something an that list she would have to sell the foal. Well, the foal was born in August. UR named him atian. Arabian, laugh ingenious, olivia, nate. UR proved to her dad that she was responsible. So the new foal can help you remember inauguration. In Aug. UR got Ation!

Amazing Alliteration

OBJECTIVE: Students experiment with alliteration and descriptive words in the style of Graeme Base's *Animalia* (Abrams, 1993).

GROUPING: Small groups of 4 to 5 students

What to Do

Read *Animalia* aloud to your class. After discussing how the author uses descriptive words and alliteration, assign each group of students two to three pages of the book to study. Each group must find the meaning of any unknown words in their section. Once the groups have defined the words, have each group read their section of the book aloud and explain the words to the class. Students then use these new words to write their own ABC books that feature descriptive words and alliteration.

Important Books

OBJECTIVE: Students explain a word by describing its key characteristics.

GROUPING: Individual

What to Do

In *The Important Book* (Harper, 1949), Margaret Wise Brown describes objects, such as a shoe, snow, and an apple, by describing what is most important about them. For example, she writes: "The important thing about a shoe is that you put your foot in it. You walk in it, and you take it off at night…" After sharing the book with the class, tell your students to pick a vocabulary word to describe using the same format. (Nouns work best for this activity.) Once they have decided on their word, they should brainstorm, using the reproducible on page 41, a list of the elements or characteristics that best describes the word. Then, students should select five points, and out of the five, select one as "the most important thing." They should incorporate the most important things into a paragraph and, echoing *The Important Book*, repeat the most important thing in the first and last sentence.

Vocabulary Plays

OBJECTIVE: Students demonstrate the meaning of new vocabulary words by writing and performing a play that incorporates the words.

GROUPING: Small groups of 4 to 6 students

Working in small groups, students write short plays that use vocabulary words in a way that either visually or dramatically tells the audience what the word means. Give students about one to two days to write their plays and then have each group perform their play in front of the class. This is a great way for students to show what they have learned about the vocabulary words—they get so excited!

Acronyms, Eponyms, and Other Wacky Words

OBJECTIVE: Student build their vocabulary while learning about word origins.

GROUPING: Small groups and whole class

What to Do

The English language is constantly changing and growing. Help students understand how new words are created and how the meaning of a word can evolve by introducing them to the following categories of words. Present one category at a time to students and then have them work in small groups to find additional examples. After collecting information about each type of word, create a class book of Wacky Words to document your findings.

Acronyms — Words made from the first letters of other words, such as ASAP and radar are acronyms. Acronyms can also be created as mnemonic devices, for example HOMES for names of the Great Lakes and NEWS for the directions on a compass (north, east, west, south). Students can display acronyms they find in acrostic form.

Coined Words and Slang Words — People coin words to fill a need, such as fax. Slang words are usually innovative or different ways of using a word. Students can compile a list of slang words they use and try to coin a few new words.

Etymology — Introduce students to etymology, the study of the history of words including their origins and changes through time. For example, the word bonfire came from the fire that was set to burn the bodies of people who died from the Bubonic Plague in the 15th century. The original meaning was bone fire. Set students on a quest to discover the history of a word. They should try to discover what country the word is from, its original meaning, as well as its meaning today.

Eponyms — As an extension of your study of word etymologies, introduce students to eponyms, or words that are derived from a name or a place. For example, tuxedos are so named because they were first worn in Tuxedo Park, NY. Have each student find one or two eponyms and share his or her findings with the class.

Palindromes — Encourage students to find as many examples as they can find of words that are spelled the same forward and backward, such as deed, otto, mom, and madam. For more palindromes, check out *Go Hang a Salami! I'm a Lasagna Hog!* by James Agee (Farrar, 1991).

Portmanteaus — Smog, splatter, and telethon are all portmanteaus, or words made by blending parts of other words. Other examples include twirl (twist and whirl), brunch (breakfast and lunch), and slosh (slop and slush). Use the reproducible on page 42 to introduce students to portmanteaus and then encourage them to create a few of their own.

The following books are good sources of eponyms and word etymologies: *A Second Browser's Dictionary* by John Ciardi (Harper and Row, 1983); *Thereby Hangs a Tale: Stories of Curious Word Origins* by Charles Funk (Harper and Row, 1985); *Morris Dictionary of Word and Phrase Origins* by William Morris and Mary Morris (Harper and Row, 1977); *I've Got Goose Pimples* by Marvin Vanoni (Morrow, 1989); and *Guppies in Tuxedos: Funny Eponyms* by Marvin Terban (Clarion, 1988).

Super Sentences

OBJECTIVE: Students translate complex words into simple English.

GROUPING: Individual or partners

What to Do

Set your students to work solving Super Sentences. Craft your Super Sentences by substituting complex words for simple words. To understand the sentence, students will need to figure out each mystery word. As students look up each word, they should write down the meaning and word pronunciation. To fully solve the sentence, they must be able to pronounce and define each word, read the sentence as it appears, and "translate" it into simpler words.

Extension Activity

Once students get the hang of Super Sentences, try Transmogrified Phrases, which are very simple expressions that have been transformed into ornate expressions with big words. For example, "Twinkle, twinkle, little star" becomes "Scintillate, scintillate, asteroid minific." You can use popular sayings, proverbs, nursery rhymes, or favorite songs for this activity. Share a few of these with your students and challenge them to create their own.

Word Contrasts

OBJECTIVE: Students compare and contrast two words in a Word Contrast paragraph.

GROUPING: Individual

What to Do

Completing a Word Contrast Paragraph (page 43) is a great way for students to explore antonyms, or words that are opposites. Pairs of opposing characteristics—such as avaricious and altruistic or passive and aggressive—work especially well with this activity. Pass out copies of the reproducible on page 43 and ask students to select two words to contrast. After placing the first word in the line beginning, "If I were," students complete the first sentence by coming up with two examples that define the word. Then they complete the paragraph with two examples that define the opposing word.

Story Hierarchy

OBJECTIVE: Students write a story incorporating a list of vocabulary words in a specific order.

GROUPING: Individual

What to Do

Students get to put on their higher level thinking hats to do this activity. Present students with a list of five to ten vocabulary words and challenge them to write a story using the words—in the same order they appear on the list. The story can be about any subject. You can also modify this activity by allowing students to use the words in any order.

Name _____

What's Important About...

1. Brainstorm all of the important things you know about _____.
Then pick the five most important characteristics and rank them in order of importance.

2. Write a paragraph that states the most important things about your word.
List the most important characteristic in the first sentence and again in the last sentence.

The important thing about . . .

_____

_____

_____

_____

_____

_____

_____

_____

But the most important thing about . . . _____

_____

_____

Portmanteaus

Portmanteaus are words that combine the meaning and sound of two words.
Can you figure out which words were combined to create the words listed below?
Pick one word from Column A and one word from Column B.

_____ + _____ = BRUNCH

_____ + _____ = CHORTLE

_____ + _____ = CONMAN

_____ + _____ = FORTNIGHT

_____ + _____ = INFOMERCIAL

_____ + _____ = MOPED

_____ + _____ = MOTEL

_____ + _____ = SMASH

_____ + _____ = SMOG

_____ + _____ = SPLATTER

_____ + _____ = SQUIGGLE

_____ + _____ = TELETHON

Column A
television
splash
squirm
information
smoke
fourteen
breakfast
confidence
motor
smack
chuckle
motor

Column B
lunch
snort
man
mash
hotel
commercial
pedal
nights
fog
spatter
wriggle
marathon

Quick Activities to Build a Very Voluminous Vocabulary

Scholastic Professional Books

Name _____

Word Contrasts

Choose two words that are opposites and use them to complete the following paragraph.
Use the example below for reference.

Example:

Words: **aggressive**   &   **passive**

If I were aggressive
I'd stretch a single into a double at my baseball game
and I'd push my way into the front of the food line.
But I wouldn't just sit and wait for people to tell me what to do
and let people bully me around.
I'd have to be passive to do that.

Words: _____ & _____

If I were _____

I'd _____

and _____.

But I ___ouldn't _____

and _____.

I'd have to be _____ to _____that.

Quick Activities to Build a Very Voluminous Vocabulary   Scholastic Professional Books

PART 4

P
Palatial
Percolate
Perseverance

Q
Quarantine
Quadrangle
Quench

R
Radiant
Rambling
Rudimentary

S
Scurry
Sediment
Substantial

T
Tactful
Tenacious
Terrain

Vocabulary Graphic Organizers

Visual Tools to Learn New Words

Word Connection Webs

OBJECTIVE: Students brainstorm words that are associated with a topic and then use a graphic organizer to categorize the words into sub-topics.

GROUPING: Individual

What to Do

Ask students to select one vocabulary word and brainstorm a list of words related to it. The words can be connected in any way, including synonyms, antonyms, examples, or references to the word in a story. After students have collected a list of words, they should break the list into categories and sort the words into each category. Students can then create a web that places each of the words on their list in a category.

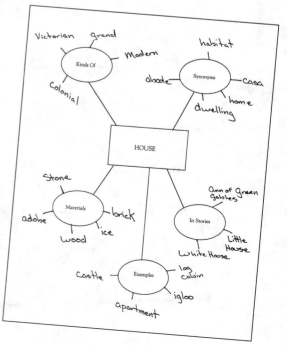

Concept Map

OBJECTIVE: Assess students' background knowledge of a topic by having them complete a Concept Map.

GROUPING: Individual

What to Do

Create a concept map using the reproducible on page 48. Place the word or concept you want students to review in the circle in the center of the page. On each of the four lines branching off the circle write a related category or topic, such as opposite words, people, or places. Then ask students to complete each section by finding words connected to each category.

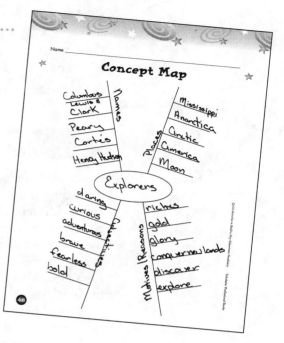

Noun Web

OBJECTIVE: Students define a noun, then brainstorm three qualities or characteristics of the noun and three examples of the noun.

GROUPING: Individual or small groups

What to Do

When students complete Noun Webs, they define a noun by describing its qualities and naming examples of it. To fill out the Noun Web reproducible on page 49, students write the noun and the definition in the large circle. Then they add three examples of the noun and three words that describe the noun. For example, if the word is Volcano, the examples might be Mt. St. Helen's, Vesuvius, and Hawaii, and the characteristics might be explosive, erupting, and lava.

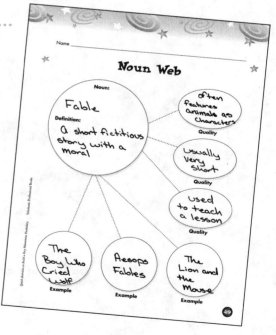

Hierarchy Word Web

OBJECTIVE: Students rank and sort words starting with the largest classes and moving to smaller classes.

GROUPING: Individual or small groups

What to Do

Hierarchy Webs are excellent ways for students to think about different classes and categories of words and work well with social studies and science topics. To create a Hierarchy Web, students begin with a large concept or word, and break the word into smaller and smaller classes. For example, if the topic is *vertebrate animals*, students could begin by listing three or four types of vertebrate animals, such as mammals, reptiles, and birds, and then branch out from each one into sub-categories, such as rodents, ocean-dwelling, and so on.

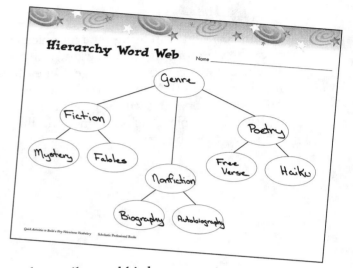

Word Venn Diagram

OBJECTIVE: Students find the similarities and differences between two words.

GROUPING: Individual

What to Do

Venn diagrams are a great way for students to compare and contrast words. For example, when learning about the government, students might draw a Venn diagram comparing *oligarchy* and *monarchy* by writing the similarities in the overlapping circles and the differences in the individual circles.

Create a Unit Web

OBJECTIVE: Students connect all the words and terms they have learned in a unit.

GROUPING: Individual or whole class

What to Do

In order for students to review all the words and concepts they have learned during a unit, create a visual map that connects everything together. As the examples below show, the webs can be simple, like the Fractions Web, or more complicated, like the Geometry Web. Creating a Unit Web as a class can be a great way to review material you have learned during a unit.

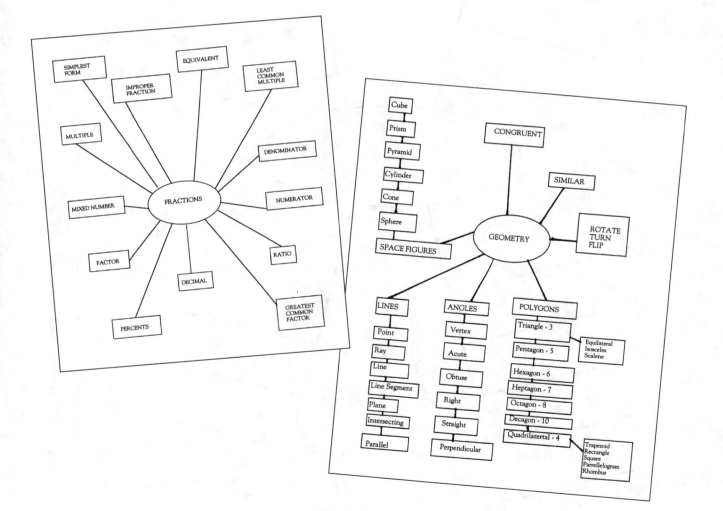

Concept Map

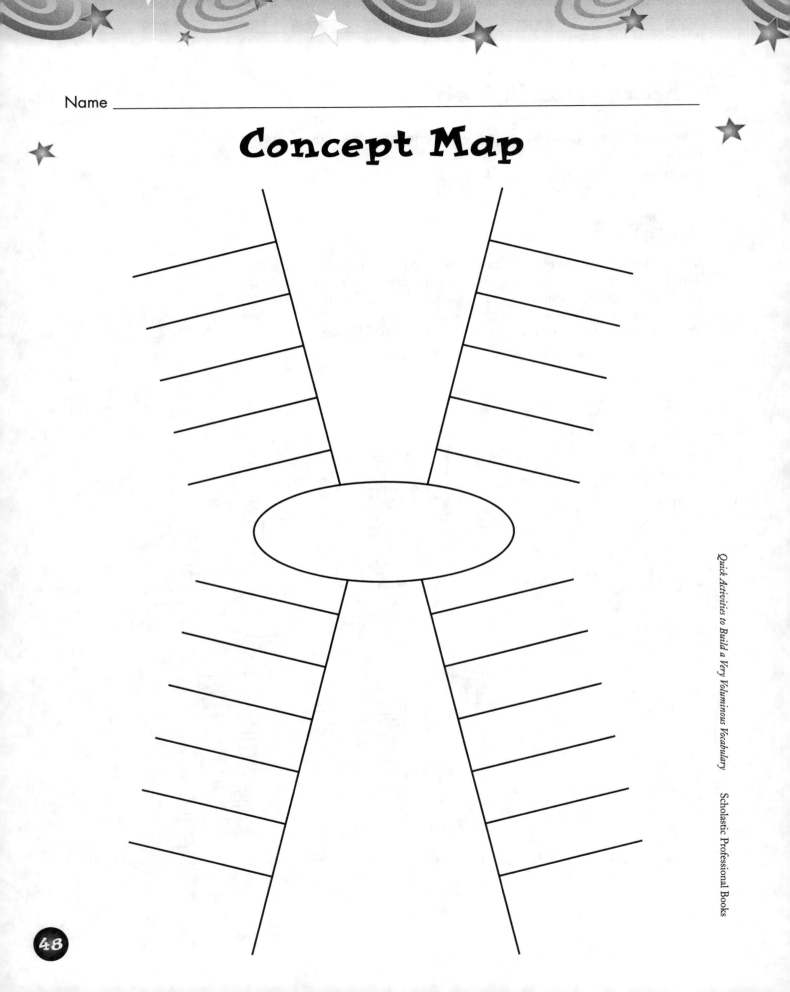

Quick Activities to Build a Very Voluminous Vocabulary   Scholastic Professional Books

Name _____

Noun Web

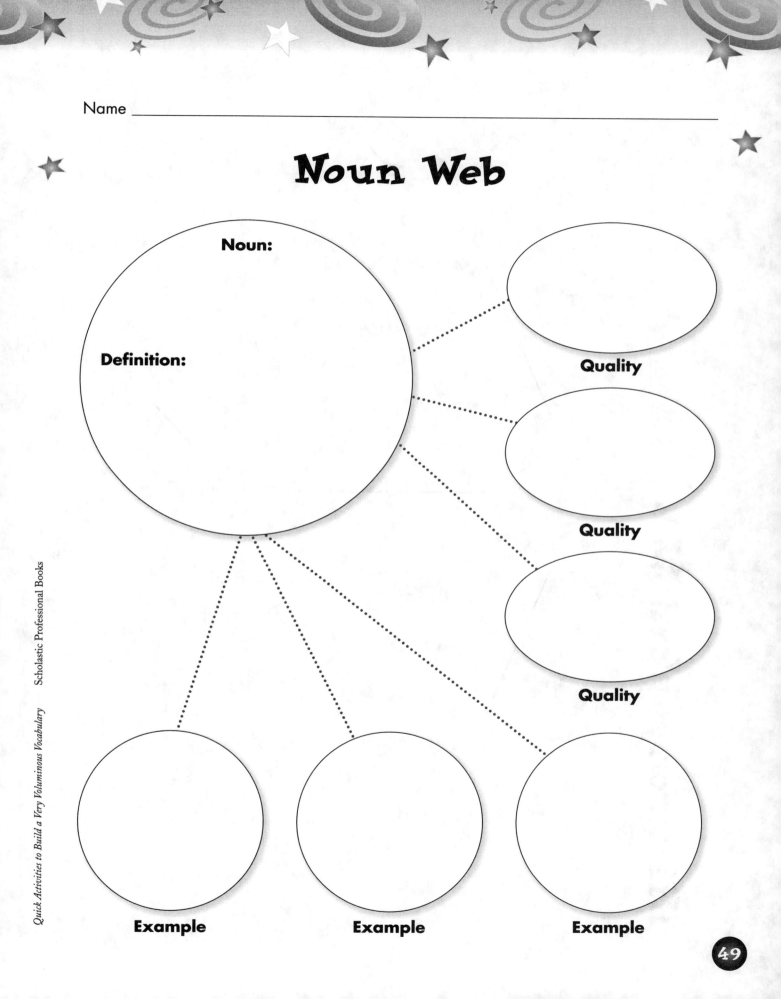

Noun:

Definition:

Quality

Quality

Quality

Example

Example

Example

Hierarchy Word Web

Name _____

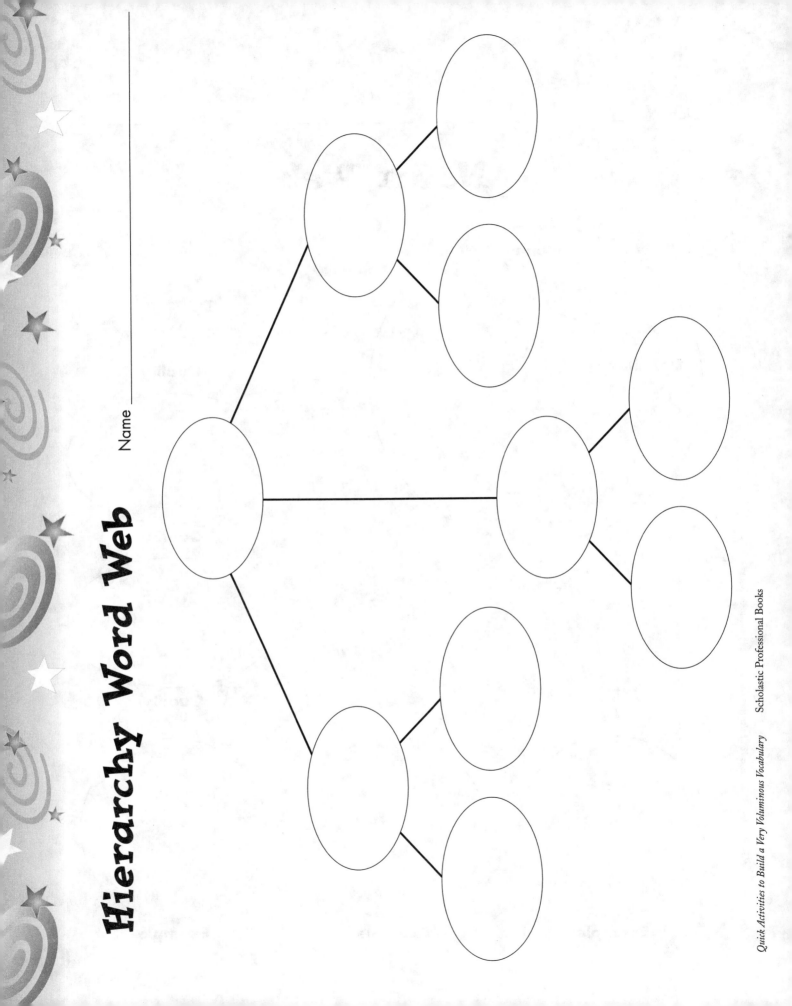

PART 5

U
Ultimatum
Umbrage
Unctuous

V
Vacillate
Vanguard
Vigilant

W
Waiver
Wizen
Wrest

XY
Xenophobe
Yammer
Yonder

Z
Zenith
Zephyr
Zest

Reviewing Vocabulary Words

Games and Activities to Help Students Remember New Words

Word Files

OBJECTIVE: Create a cumulative record of vocabulary words to help students learn and review vocabulary during the year.

GROUPING: Individual

What to Do

Keeping a word file is a great way for students to continually review vocabulary words. As you study new vocabulary in class, have students write each word on an index card. On the back of the card, have students write a definition of the word, the part of speech, and a sentence using the word. Students can store the cards in alphabetical order in a file box.

I have my students make a new set of word cards at the beginning of each unit. They work together in small groups to look up the words in the dictionary. Then they add the cards to their file. We use the cards for many vocabulary games (see following section) and, at the end of every month, students review all of the words in their file.

Students can also make word files by punching holes in index cards and clipping them together with binder rings, writing words on scrap paper and using a shoe box for a file, or storing word cards in envelopes.

Word Walls

Brick Word Wall

OBJECTIVE: Create a display devoted to vocabulary words.
GROUPING: Whole class

What to Do

It's useful for students to continually see the new words they are learning and a vocabulary Word Wall is a great way to do this. I make a very simple Brick Word Wall by hanging a large sheet of red bulletin board paper on the wall. As we learn new words, I write them on pieces of self-sticking note paper and post them on the wall. As the year progresses, we build a bigger and bigger wall.

Help with Homophones and Homonyms

OBJECTIVE: Reinforce the meaning of homophone and homonym pairs.
GROUPING: Whole class

What to Do

Even middle school students still have trouble with homophones. To remind students to use the correct words, I create a Homophone Help Board. I post the homophone pairs and sentences using the words on the wall. Students can add to and refer to the display when they are writing.

Thematic Bulletin Boards

OBJECTIVE: Design theme-based bulletin boards that feature vocabulary words.

GROUPING: Whole class

What to Do

Thematic Bulletin Boards are a great way to display new vocabulary words. I design bulletin boards related to the subject for students to label with vocabulary words. For example, during our unit on space, we created a large display of our solar system. As we learned new words, students added labels to the display. Students can use the bulletin board for reference during the unit.

Vocabulary Games

Off Limits

OBJECT: In this game, inspired by the popular game Taboo, players try to guess a target word after hearing the word described.

PLAYERS: Two teams

To Prepare

Give each student an index card with a vocabulary word written on it. Ask students to write five words that describe or relate to the vocabulary word on the card. These words are off-limits and can't be used during the game. Collect the cards.

To Play

Divide the class into two teams. To start the game, a student from one team picks a card and gives his teammates clues to the word without using any of the off-limits words on the card. The team has one minute to guess the word and earn one point for each word they correctly guess. If the team member says any of the words that are off-limits, the other team wins a point.

What's Missing?

OBJECT: A concentration-style game in which students try to guess which word is missing and then define the missing word.

PLAYERS: Whole class

To Play

Use this activity to sharpen students' visual memories while reviewing vocabulary words. Write the unit words on index cards and tape them to the chalkboard. Have students study the words that are on the board for two to three minutes. Then ask students to close their eyes while you remove one card from the board. Challenge students to guess the missing word and then define it.

Homonym Tag

OBJECT: Review the spelling and meaning of homonyms.

PLAYERS: Two teams, Team A and Team B

To Prepare

Copy the list of homonyms on page 61.

To Play

Display the list of homonyms on an overhead transparency, or make copies of the list for the entire class. To begin playing, a student from team A chooses a homonym and spells the word out loud. A member of team B must then use the word correctly in a sentence. If the team B member uses the word correctly, he or she picks another homonym from the list and challenges a member from team A to use the word in a sentence. If the team B member is incorrect, the team A member continues calling on team B members until they answer correctly. Place a check mark beside the homonym after it is used.

Looping Game

OBJECT: Match vocabulary words with their definitions.

PLAYERS: Whole class

To Prepare

Make copies of the Looping Game cards on page 59. Prepare the game cards by writing the definitions of your vocabulary words under "I have." Then, keeping the cards in the same order, write in the "Who has" section of each card, the vocabulary word that fits the definition on the card in front of it.

After handing every student in class a card, the first person starts the game by saying, "Who has … [vocabulary word]." Students read their card to see if the definition under "I have" fits the word. The person with the matching definition says, "I have…," reads the definition and continues the loop by saying, "Who has …[vocabulary word]." If the game works correctly, the last person will say, "Who has…[vocabulary word]" and the person who started the game will finally say his or her "I have" statement. Every person has to be alert in order to catch their turn and continue the loop.

Name That Word

OBJECT: Students name a word after hearing identifying clues.

PLAYERS: Two teams

To Prepare

To create the game cards you will need for this exercise, give each team a set of vocabulary words. Then, using the following prompts, each team writes seven clues on an index card for each vocabulary word:

Clue #1: Part of speech
Clue #2: Use the word in a sentence (word left blank)
Clue #3: Antonym
Clue #4: Synonym
Clue #5: Number of syllables
Clue #6: Starts like … or sounds like …
Clue #7: A giveaway clue—pronunciation clues, rhymes with, etc.

To Play

The two teams exchange sets of clue cards. Each team tries to guess the other team's vocabulary words based on the seven clues. The team with the most correct guesses wins!

Alternative

You can also play Name That Word as a class. Have each student in your class write a clue card for one vocabulary word and then collect all the cards. Select one card and start to read the clues aloud. The first student to raise her hand while you're reading the clues gets to guess what the word might be. If the guess is incorrect, continue reading the rest of the clues for that word until someone guesses correctly.

Word Tic-Tac-Toe

OBJECT: Players win tic-tac-toe spaces by correctly defining vocabulary words.

PLAYERS: Pairs

To Prepare

Create tic-tac-toe grids with a vocabulary word in each square.

To Play

Divide the class into pairs and give each pair a tic-tac-toe grid. Players must correctly define the word before putting an "X" or an "O" in the spot. The first player to get three in a row wins the game.

Vocabulary Concentration

OBJECT: Match vocabulary words with their definitions.

PLAYERS: Pairs or small groups

To Prepare

Select 15 words for review. Write each word on an index card and then write the definition of each word on a separate index card.

To Play

Shuffle the cards and place them face down on a table. Each player takes turns flipping over two cards to find a vocabulary word and the matching definition. If the cards don't match, players turn them face down again. If the cards do match, players can take the pair. Players who make a match may go again. At the end of the game, the player with the greatest number of pairs wins.

Alternatives

Players can also try to match words that are synonyms, antonyms, or homonyms.

Wordo Bingo

OBJECT: Students win bingo by completing sentences with the correct vocabulary word.

PLAYERS: Whole class

To Prepare

Write 25 fill-in-the-blank sentences using vocabulary words you want to review with your students. The sentences will need to feature context clues to help students identify which vocabulary word they should use to fill in the blank.

To Play

Make copies of the Wordo card on page 60 and distribute the cards to your students. Display the 25 vocabulary words and have students fill in the spaces on their Wordo card—in any order they please—with the words. Then, begin to read each fill-in-the-blank sentence to the class. As you read, students place a marker (bean, noodle, candy, etc.) on the vocabulary word that would complete that sentence correctly. The first player to score five words in a row—horizontally, diagonally, or vertically—wins the game. (You can also play this game by showing students the sentences—with the vocabulary words missing, of course—on an overhead transparency.)

Tell Me About Myself

OBJECT: Students try to identify a mystery vocabulary word taped to their back by asking questions.

PLAYERS: Whole class

To Prepare

Write vocabulary words on blank index cards. You'll need a card for every student in your class.

To Play

Pin or tape an index card with a vocabulary word on it to the back of each student. Students must figure out which word is on their back by circulating around the room, asking other students questions. Each question must begin with "Tell me about myself," and must have a yes or no answer. Questions might include: "Am I an adjective?" "Do I begin with a vowel?" The entire class wins when everybody has figured out their word.

Sentence Sense

OBJECT: Students try to use as many vocabulary words as they can in one sentence.

PLAYERS: Whole class

To Play

List five to seven vocabulary words on the board and challenge students to use as many words as they can in one complete, sensible sentence. Students can read their sentences aloud after they have completed them. You can vary the number of words according to players' abilities.

Puzzle Charades

OBJECT: Students win puzzle pieces by correctly guessing words.

PLAYERS: Teams of 5 to 6 students.

To Prepare

Begin by making a puzzle for each team. To create the puzzles, laminate colorful pictures and cut into pieces. Place the pieces to each puzzle in a separate bag. Write 10 to 20 vocabulary words on index cards.

To Play

Give each team a bag with the pieces of one puzzle. Start the game by having a member of one team pick a vocabulary word and silently act it out. Allow the actor's team 3 minutes to guess the word. If the team guesses, the actor selects one puzzle piece and adds it to the team's puzzle. Then the team chooses a new actor and goes again. If a team doesn't guess correctly, the play rotates to the next team. The team that completes its puzzle first wins.

Crossword Puzzles

OBJECT: Students create crossword puzzles using vocabulary words.

PLAYERS: Individual

To Play

Crossword puzzles are an easy way for student to practice using vocabulary. Students select 15 to 20 words for their puzzles and write clues based on the definitions, synonyms, or antonyms. Give students sheets of graph paper to create their puzzles. Students can exchange completed crosswords.

Looping Game

Cut the cards apart on the dotted line.

I have:

Who has:

I have:

Who has:

I have:

Who has:

I have:

Who has:

I have:

Who has:

I have:

Who has:

Wordo

Name _____

Homonyms

billed, build

bored, board

break, brake

by, buy, bye

capital, capitol

ceiling, sealing

cell, sell

cent, sent, scent

compliment, complement

creak, creek

dear, deer

die, dye

flour, flower

for, four, fore

hair, hare

hay, hey

heard, herd

heel, heal, he'll

hole, whole

horse, hoarse

hour, our

knead, need

knight, night

lesson, lessen

meat, meet

new, knew, gnu

no, know

not, knot

one, won

pail, pale

pain, pane

pair, pear, pare

peak, peek

piece, peace

plain, plane

presents, presence

principle, principal

past, passed

patients, patience

pause, paws

rain, reign, rein

raise, rays, raze

read, red

right, write, rite

road, rode

role, roll

sail, sale

scene, seen

sea, see

sew, so, sow

sighed, side

sight, site, cite

some, sum

stair, stare

steak, stake

straight, strait

tale, tail

they're, there, their

threw, through

to, too, two

toe, tow

wade, weighed

waste, waist

week, weak

wood, would

wring, ring

50 Common Affixes & Roots

1. AB – *away from*
  abnormal – away from normal (adj.)
  abandon – draw away from (v.)

2. AN – *without*
  anarchy – without a ruler (n.)
  anonymous – without a name (adj.)

3. ANTI – *against*
  antibiotic – against a living virus (n)
  anti–Semitic – against Hebrews (adj.)

4. ANTE – *before*
  ante-bellum – before the Civil War (adj.)
  antedate – come before in time (v.)

5. ANTHROPO – *man*
  anthropology – study of mankind (n.)
  philanthropist – lover of mankind (n.)

6. AQUA – *water*
  aquarium – holds water and fish (n.)
  aquamarine – color of water (n.)

7. AUTO – *self*
  autobiography – self–written life story (n.)
  automatic – operating by itself (adj.)

8. ARCH – *chief*
  anarchy – without a chief (n.)
  archrival – chief rival (n.)

9. ASTRO – *star*
  astronomy – study of the stars (n.)
  astronaut – someone who travels around the stars (n.)

10. BI – *two*
  bikini – two piece bathing suit (n.)
  bicycle – two-wheel cycle (n.)

11. BIO – *life*
  biology – study of life (n.)
  biography – written life story (n.)

12. CIRCUM – *around*
  circumference – measure around a circle (n.)
  circumvent – surround (v.)

13. COL – *together*
  collect – gather together (v.)
  colony – a group living together (n.)

14. COM – *together*
  commune – live together (v.)
  combine – put together (v.)

15. CON – *together*
  congregate – group together (v.)
  connect – join together (v.)

16. CONTRA – *against*
  contrary – against something (adj.)
  contradict – speak against something (v.)

17. COSMO – *world*
  cosmology – study of the origin of the world (n.)
  cosmopolitan – of the entire world (adj.)

18. CRACY – *rule/government*
  democracy – rule by the people (n.)
  autocracy – rule by one person (n.)

19. DE – *to make less*
  deduct – subtract from (v.)
  degrade – take worth from (v.)

20. DICT – *say*
  diction – the way something is said (n.)
  dictation – the writing of what is said (n.)

21. EXTRA – *beyond/outside*
  extracurricular – beyond the curriculum (adj.)
  extravagant – beyond the budget (adj.)

22. EX – *out*
  exit – go out (v.)
  expire – breathe out (v.)

23. GEO – *earth*
  geography – study of the places of the earth (n.)
  geology – study of the elements of the earth (n.)

24. GRAPH – *something written or drawn*
  graphology – study of handwriting (n.)
  autograph – self-written name (n.)

25. HEMI – *half*
    hemisphere – half of the world (n.)
    hemicycle – half a cycle (n.)

26. HOMO – *same*
    homogenized – the same throughout (adj.)
    homographs – words written the same (n.)

27. HYDRO – *water*
    hydrant – holds water (n.)
    dehydrate – remove water from (v.)

28. JECT – *throw*
    reject – throw away (v.)
    projectile – something that is thrown (n.)

29. MACRO – *large*
    macrocosm – the universe (n.)
    macroscopic – seen without a microscope (adj.)

30. MATRI – *mother*
    maternal – motherly (adj.)
    matriarch – a woman who rules (n.)

31. METER – *measure*
    thermometer – measure of heat (n.)
    speedometer – measures speed (n.)

32. MICRO – *small*
    microcosm – small world (n.)
    microorganism – small organism (n.)

33. MIS – *wrong/bad*
    misbehave – behavior wrongly (v.)
    misprint – wrong printing (v)

34. MONO – *one/single*
    monogamy – having one wife (n.)
    monologue – one person talk (n.)

35. ONYM – *name*
    homonym – same name (n.)
    antonym – opposite name (n.)

36. OB – *against*
    object – speak against (v.)
    obstacle – something which goes against progress (n.)

37. PAN – *all*
    panorama – view of all things (n.)
    pandemic – affecting all things (adj.)

38. PATRI – *father*
    paternity – related to fatherhood (adj.)
    patriarch – a man who rules a family (n.)

39. PERI – *around*
    perimeter – measurement around (n.)
    periphery – the edge around (n.)

40. PER – *through*
    permeate – soak through (v.)
    perforate – put holes through (v.)

41. PHILE, PHIL – *lover of*
    philosophy – love of wisdom (n.)
    audiophile – lover of sound (n.)

42. POLY – *many*
    polytheism – belief in many gods (n.)
    monopoly – one who owns many (n.)

43. PORT – *carry*
    transport – carry across (v.)
    portable – able to be carried (adj.)

44. POST – *after*
    postpone – change date to a later date (v.)
    posthumous – after death (adj.)

45. PRO – *before/forward*
    provide – give something before it is needed (n.)
    prophecy – knowledge before of what will happen (n.)

46. PSEUDO – *false*
    pseudonym – false name (n.)
    pseudoscience – false science (n.)

47. PSYCH – *mind*
    psychiatry – healing of the mind (n.)
    psyche – mind or soul (n.)

48. PRE – *before*
    preview – see before (v.)
    precede – come before (v.)

49. RE – *again*
    return – go back again (v.)
    reunite – unite again (v.)

50. SEMI – *half*
    semiannual – every half year (adj.)
    semicircle – half–circle (n.)

Bibliography

Anders, Patricia L., and Candace Bos . "Semantic Feature Analysis: An Interactive Strategy for Vocabulary Development and Text Comprehension." *Journal of Reading* (April 1986): 610–615.

Blachowicz, Camille L Z. "Making Connections: Alternatives to the Vocabulary Notebook." *Journal of Reading* (April 1986): 643–649.

Blachowicz, Camille L.Z. and John J. Lee. "Vocabulary Development in the Whole Literacy Classroom." *The Reading Teacher* (November 1991): 188–194.

Buikema, Janice L. and Michael F. Graves. "Teaching Students to Use Context Cues to Infer Word Meanings." *Journal of Reading* (March 1993): 450–456.

Cudd, Evelyn T. and Leslie L. Roberts. "A Scaffolding Technique to Develop Sentence Sense and Vocabulary." *The Reading Teacher* (Dec/Jan 1994).

Macon, James M.; Diane Bewell; and MaryEllen Vogt, (1991). *Responses to Literature.* (International Reading Association, 1991)

Macmillan/McGraw Hill. *A to EZ Handbook: Staff Development Guide.* (MacMillan & McGraw-Hill, 1993).

Nagy, William E. *Vocabulary to Improve Reading Comprehension.* (International Reading Association, 1988).

Nagy, William E. and Patricia A. Herman. "Incidental vs. Instructional Approaches to Increasing Reading Vocabulary." *Educational Perspectives* (1985): pp. 16–21.

Stahl, Steven and Barbara A. Kapinus . "Possible Sentences: Predicting Word Meanings to Teach Content Area Vocabulary." *The Reading Teacher* (Sept. 1991) pp. 36–42.

Sutton, Rebecca. *Rebecca Sutton's Spelling Sourcebook.* (Curriculum Associates, 1995).

Winebrenner, Susan. *Teaching Gifted Kids in the Regular Classroom.* (Free Spirit Publishing Inc., 1992).